Follow That Boat!
A Story Book

by Jim Razzi
illustrated by Paul Richer

Here comes a big boat called an ocean liner.
Where is it going?
Let's follow it and see.

It goes into the harbor.
Its big horns are blowing.
It is bringing back passengers
from a vacation trip.
The big boat passes a ferryboat.

Let's follow that ferryboat and see where it goes!

It goes to a large island on the other side of the harbor.
All the passengers and cars get off.
Then more passengers and cars get on.
And back goes the ferry.
Back and forth—all day long.

The captain of the ferryboat
sees a lightship coming.
The captain of the lightship
is his friend.
Toot! Toot! He blows his whistle
to say hello.

7

"Hello," the lightship answers
with a blast from its foghorn.

Let's follow that lightship
and see where it goes.

It goes out to sea near the entrance
to the harbor.
There is no place to build a lighthouse there.
The lightship is a floating lighthouse!
The light helps the sailors
find their way at night.

Look!
Here comes a fishing boat.
Let's follow that fishing boat
and see where it goes.

It goes out to sea where all the fish are.
Soon the crew spots a school of fish!
"Hooray!" they shout.
Two small boats go out with a big net
to catch the fish.
Then a pilot boat chugs by.

Let's follow that pilot boat
and see where it goes.

It goes alongside a freighter
carrying cargo from far away.
A man from the pilot boat climbs
aboard the freighter.

FREIGHTER

He's the pilot who will guide the big
freighter safely to the dock.
That's where the cargo
will be unloaded.

As the freighter is piloted into the harbor,
a fireboat comes dashing by.
It cuts through the water making two big
waves.
"Whooo! Whooo!" goes its siren.
"Get out of the way!"

Let's follow that fireboat
and see where it goes!

It goes to a wooden pier.
A small fire is burning there.
It started in a trash can.
If it is not put out quickly,
it will become a big fire!

The fireboat comes right up to the pier and stops.
The firemen work fast.
The boat pumps water from the harbor and aims it at the fire.
The fire is out in no time!

Some of the water sprays a tugboat that passes.
"Hey!" yells a man on the deck.
"I already took my shower today.
I'm getting all wet!"
He laughs and waves at the firemen.

Where is the tugboat going?
Let's follow it and see.

It goes to a dock where it picks up a barge
full of coal.
The tugboat is very strong.
It can tow a big ocean liner.
It can tow boats ten times bigger than itself.

Just as the crew settles down for the ride,
the tugboat passes a small houseboat.
"Hello there!" shouts a family on the houseboat.
They are hanging out their wash.
Let's follow that houseboat and see where it goes.

It goes up a small canal.
The houseboat passes a small sailboat.
"Happy sailing," the family yells.

Let's follow that sailboat and see where it goes.

It goes to a big dock where there are
lots of other sailboats.
All the captains know one another.
They sit and talk just like next-door neighbors.

All of a sudden, a speedboat zips by.
Look! It's pulling a water skier.

The skier does all kinds of tricks on her skis.
Zoom! She passes a little rowboat.
The rowboat bobs up and down from the waves.

The people in the rowboat wave to the skier.
Then they keep rowing up the canal.
Where are they going?
Let's follow them and see.

It is getting dark.
It is time to row
that boat...

all the way home.